Losing Emily

A JOURNEY THROUGH STILLBIRTH TO FINDING PEACE AND EMBRACING NEW HOPE

TAMMY ANDERSON

PORTLAND • OREGON
INKWATERPRESS.COM

618.
32
A

The information contained in this book was the sole experience of the author and was not intended to replace professional assistance or guidance.

Additional copies available by sending cheque/ money order for $16.95 US / $18.95 CND plus $3.00 shipping to:

T. Anderson
Box 1723
Jasper, Alberta, Canada
TOE 1E0

or please visit:
www.inkwaterbooks.com

Copyright © 2010 by Tammy Anderson

Cover and interior design by Mindy Holt

© Stuart Miles. Image from BigStockPhoto.com

www.inkwaterpress.com

ISBN-13 978-1-59299-460-1
ISBN-10 1-59299-460-1

Publisher: Inkwater Press

Printed in the U.S.A.
All paper is acid free and meets all ANSI standards for archival quality paper.

3 5 7 9 10 8 6 4 2

In loving memory of our beautiful little girl

Emily Megan Anderson

Stillborn on May 10th, 2006
6 pounds, 9 ounces

Although you are not here with us, you are in our hearts always, missed deeply and loved forever.

INTRODUCTION

If you are reading this, I imagine you are going through every parent's worst nightmare; you have lost a precious child or know someone in your life who is going through this horrific devastation and heartache. The pain and shock of having to say goodbye to your beautiful baby before you have even had a chance to say hello is unimaginable to anyone who has not lived through it. I am so deeply sorry, I truly understand because I too have travelled down that dark and lonely road.

In 2006, my husband and I lost a baby girl to stillbirth at 37.5 weeks of pregnancy. Since then I have often reflected back on the early days of returning home from the hospital and the burning desire to get my hands on any kind of reading material to answer the millions of questions running through my mind. Desperate for answers, I spent countless hours scouring the internet, as well as the library catalog. There was not much out there that I could find. Alot of the material was written more from a medical perspective rather than focusing on feelings or making a connection with someone living through the loss of a child. It left me feeling alone and confused.

I often thought of putting my thoughts and healing into words, and creating a book to share with others trying to find a way to live through this, who are seeking comfort from others who truly understand. Over and over I thought, why would anyone want to read about a 34–year–old educational assistant from a small Alberta town and the loss of her baby, a thing that happens to countless others everyday all over the world? Albeit the loss of a child or pregnancy at any stage is horrendous and cruel. I feel it important to mention that I do not, in any way, feel that my story or loss is any more important than anyone else's. Each precious baby has a special story to tell. Every tiny life deserves to be treasured, shared and remembered.

Looking back at the lack of support I felt and my deep rooted desire to find a connection, more solid information on our baby's death and the mystery and anguish surrounding it, led me to pursue the 'birth' of this book.

It is my hope that you find some comfort in my story. If my words can reach out and send a message of peace, a connection to just one person in need, then my wish has truly been fulfilled. Know that you are not alone in this journey through the powerful grieving process.

CHAPTER 1

After a very difficult time in my life (the summer of 2002), I found myself and my two young children alone as I went through a totally unexpected divorce. Unsure of what the future would bring, I went about my days doing everything for my kids, putting them first and enjoying everything with them. We had each other and drew strength and comfort in moving forward as a little family unit. We persevered through many tough times and received unconditional love and support from my mom, who thankfully lives nearby. She provided us with assistance, both financially and emotionally, because she knew I was struggling. I will never be able to repay her for all she has done. She has been there and helped out, not saying a word, simply because she knew we needed it.

One Friday evening, I had the rare bliss of a night out with some friends, thanks to my wonderfully supportive mom, who offered babysitting so I could go out. At the local pub, I bumped into a man whom I had known for many years. He was there with a group of co–workers and friends, unwinding at happy hour. I was enjoying the night out and the casual chatter amongst friends, when I noticed that he had moved over to join our boisterous table. We talked briefly, reminiscing about the past and catching up. As he had to work the early shift at the grocery store, where he worked as the bakery department manager, he had to cut the evening short.

The next day while I was working at a part time seasonal job, Darren came by and asked me out on a date! During a quiet, romantic dinner we talked easily about our lives, jobs and children. Beaming, he told me about his son, a 20–year–old successful oil field worker. On the way home we stopped by his house as he had something he wanted to show me. In his small, cozy living room there were several photos of his son that he proudly showed off to me. A while later, I finally was able to meet him and see what a kind and gentle young man he was! To say he was awesome would be an understatement!

Although we don't get to see him as much as we would like, it makes the times we do have together all the more special to us. Distance may separate us, but we look so forward to spending any time we can with him.

Many months went by and Darren and I grew closer, and I was able to fully appreciate just what an amazing man I was dating.

Together Darren and I, growing increasingly more confident in the strength of our flourishing relationship, slowly began including my children on our outings. I was fiercely protective of them and was ever so careful not to expose them to anyone in their lives who would leave and cause them any heartache again.

It was several months before Darren joined us one day to go skating on a beautiful outdoor lake nearby in the serenity of our mountain paradise. There were many laughs as the four of us played together all afternoon. We grew to love his kind, loving and caring heart and welcomed him into our family.

He was not their father, but loved and cared for them more deeply as each day passed.

Not long afterwards, I was introduced to his family on a trip we all took into Edmonton. Everyone in his family; from his parents to his brother and sisters and their families, welcomed us and treated us like one of their own.

I felt truly blessed.

Months passed into years and we were engaged on New Year's Eve, 2003! We were married on a beautiful island just outside of Jasper on July 24th, 2004. The day was breathtakingly hot, with not a cloud in the sky. Surrounded by our families and close friends, whom we loved dearly, I married my best friend. It was the start of a new chapter for all of us and we looked forward to many new adventures together.

CHAPTER 2

We had often talked about the desire we both felt to have one more baby, a child who would be a part of both of us and complete our new family.

In September of 2005, after getting several negative pregnancy tests, I still felt with a mother's intuition, the knowing drive, that I really *was* pregnant; no matter what it said on the stick. No words could express how excited I was to see the second line confirming a positive pregnancy on an HPT(Home Pregnancy Test)! I was elated, grateful to be starting this new chapter and excited about being a new mommy again.

My pregnancy had its share of ups and downs but the baby was healthy during all early check ups and ultrasounds. Our local hospital no longer did any deliveries, which meant all the pregnant mommies had to drive 45 minutes down the highway to a larger hospital better equipped for the special needs of labor and delivery. This hospital was also equipped with an ultrasound machine, something that was not available at our local facility.

I was surprised that I was feeling so good, as my other two pregnancies had left me feeling terribly nauseous for the entire nine months. For me, it wasn't morning sickness, but all day sickness! This time I was tired, but still able to work. I remember having the luxury of coming home and being able to lay on the couch when I felt I needed. My loving, fantastic husband cooked dinner and took care of the kids after school activities so I could rest. My life felt perfect, I went through my daily routine of work, attending various functions with my children, and relishing in the new life growing inside me.

In December, we received a phone call from my mom saying she didn't feel well, and wanted to go to the emergency room. Now you have to know that my mom didn't like going to the doctor, never thought she had to. Now she was asking for me to take her to the hospital. I knew immediately that something was *really* wrong. She'd spent most of that day at home, in and out of sleep until she'd mustered up the strength to call me. I rushed over and had to help her to the car. She was deathly white, her lips were blue and she could hardly stand up. I raced the couple of blocks to the emergency room, my heart filled with fear.

They rushed her into the trauma room and hooked her up to the heart monitor, she was awake and responsive to their questions. The doctor then told her that she had had a heart attack. After the preliminary assessment she was stabilized and taken by ambulance to a mediplane that would rush her to Edmonton to see a cardiology specialist.

Darren and I made frantic arrangements with wonderful friends to look after my children so we could drive in and be with her. I remember walking into that huge hospital, the smell nauseating, my heart racing. Mom had regained her color and was feeling a lot better. She was scheduled to be taken to another hospital the following day to have stints put in her blocked arteries.

We returned home that night and had plans to return again in a few days. After calling the hospital all day and not being able to get any answers of how the operation went, I became very concerned. Finally, after several more frantic phone calls to the hospital, I managed to track down the nurse taking care of her and was told that she had "crashed" during the procedure. It was very serious, and she told us to come right away. Once again, our dear friends came to the rescue by taking my children as we rushed back the four hours to the city.

When we arrived, Mom was on a breathing

tube and heavily medicated. She opened her eyes when we came to the bed and nodded in response to our questions. She wrote things down on a clipboard and we would answer her. We spent about five days there with her, as each day passed she became stronger until the doctor agreed to release her to the hospital here in Jasper. It was Christmas and this would allow her to be close to our family and her friends.

One awesome moment occurred while we were in the waiting room outside the CCU one day. It was the first time I was able to feel my tiny baby kick, almost as if to say, "I'm here, everything's going to be ok."

That Christmas we had so much to be thankful for, above all my mom's recovery and having her at home with us. A scare for us that made me to this day grateful for even the simplest of things that I took for granted on a daily basis, we were truly blessed.

CHAPTER 3

The new year rang in and we found ourselves anxiously awaiting the pregnancy to draw to a close and dreamed of finally seeing our baby, this active little kicker growing inside me. We anticipated and dreamed of a lifetime of watching the baby grow and change. We'd had another ultrasound and were able to see that this little one was a girl! So I, of course, had gone out and bought pink; two hundred and fifty dollars worth of pink sleepers, dresses, blankets, pink soothers, pink flowery bibs!

I was ready. I knew the end was nearing and I was making the final preparations to bring this baby home at last. My husband's parents had hand crafted a gorgeous pine cradle for her that had been placed at the foot of our bed. The delicate little pink clothes were all washed and lovingly placed in the dresser, the hospital bag packed with all our necessities, everything was ready for the big moment to arrive. Everything was falling neatly into place. Now all we had to do was wait . . .

In approximately my thirty-fourth week of pregnancy, I woke to this very odd sensation on the right side of my face. It started on my tongue; I felt like I had just been to the dentist and had the freezing in my mouth. Then it progressed to kind of an achy feeling in my right cheek. Later in the afternoon, as we were in the doctor's office, she told me I was not blinking my right eye!

After a phone consultation with a specialist in the city I was told I had Bell's Palsy! The doctor prescribed me a steroid which I was very leery of taking, terrified of any complications that would harm my baby girl in any way. I was assured it would do no harm so, *VERY* reluctantly I began the treatment. I did not notice any major changes to my face until after the birth. Slowly, I was able to blink my eye again.

To this day when I have been laughing or smiling for any long period of time, the right side of my face will ache temporarily, a constant reminder of the beginning of a very dark time for me.

CHAPTER 4

Two weeks later we went to what I had hoped was one of our last prenatal appointments. The mood in the room was light and we had agreed that the baby would come by induction that Friday. My doctor did the internal exam and then took out the doppler to listen to the baby's heart . . . nothing could have prepared me for what would happen next; in a split second my life would be changed forever.

The doctor gently slid the doppler across my now bulging belly. She did this a few times, with each swipe I could see the look of concern on her face become more intense. She asked me to roll over and change position thinking that perhaps the baby was sleeping or just nestled in a funny position. Finally after what seemed like an eternity to me . . . I heard a *thump–thump–thump* . . . I remember saying to her, "Whew, ok that was scary!" She looked at my husband and I and said, "No that's you, I can't find the baby's heartbeat." She did her best to try to reassure me saying that maybe it could just be a faulty doppler. As a precaution, she wanted me to go to the hospital and be hooked up to the fetal monitors. I don't remember a lot of what happened on the way there. I wanted only to believe it was not true, these terrible things happened to other people, not to me.

We arrived mere minutes later and the nurses had everything ready to go. After a few tries, they were not able to find a trace of our little girl's heartbeat. I lay on the bed in complete and utter shock. I knew and understood what they were telling me, but I couldn't feel anything at that moment. My doctor arrived then and confirmed *fetal demise*. We were asked to return to the hospital first thing in the morning for an ultrasound to confirm the evident.

I could not sleep at all that night, to try was pointless. I remember laying there in my bed, watching the minutes turn into hours, willing with all my heart for my baby to be still alive, for the doctor to be wrong; praying that it was all just a terrible mistake.

At 7:30 the following morning, I lay on that same table, in that same darkened room. The room that I had once marvelled at, on that very screen, this wondrous little life moving around. Now we saw only a still, lifeless image. I heard the technician say those awful words, "I am afraid the doctor's diagnosis is correct, there is no heartbeat. All the chambers in the heart have shut down. I am so very sorry."

We walked down the long corridor, everything a blur. I felt like there was a thick black fog surrounding me. I felt nauseous.

We were ushered into a room where we waited for my doctor to arrive and tell us what we already knew. She was very matter of fact, giving us two options: I could wait no more than two weeks and labor would begin on its own, or I could come back tomorrow and be induced. I immediately told her, "I want you to do a C-Section, take the baby out." I didn't want to prolong the process and wanted the baby out quickly. She refused adamantly saying that because I had been prescribed steroids with the Bell's Palsy there was a greater chance of infection from the wound site; plus that the healing will be quicker if I gave birth naturally. We left the hospital that cool spring morning in May and embarked on the drive back home.

My thoughts then raced to my concern over how was I going to tell the kids that the baby sister they had waited for so anxiously was gone and would never be coming home. How could they be expected to understand this and the impact it would have on their lives as well? We encouraged them both to ask whatever questions they had. Although we didn't have all the answers. We could only tell them what we were told, that no one really knows why, that it was a terrible accident, the baby's heart stopped beating and she was gone. We told them it was nothing anyone did or didn't do but that she had died inside of mommy's belly. They wanted more information, some solid facts to help them understand why their sister was never coming home. To this day they still think about her and something will trigger their curiosity about how old she would be now or what she would be like.

Initially it was too painful for me to talk about at all, with anyone, and Darren would sit with the kids and lovingly answer their questions sometimes over and over again as best he could. Whatever we could do to help them get through this, we did our best.

We decided the next day that we needed to go ahead and induce and begin the healing process. For in waiting we would be not be given the bliss of a healthy baby at the end of the road. We called the doctor's office and she agreed to meet us first thing the next morning.

CHAPTER 5

After making arrangements to have my mom once again stay and look after the kids, we dropped the two children off at school and began the now familiar journey back to the hospital, this time to begin the induction. The entire way through misted eyes and still reeling in shock, I thought to myself, *how am I going to deliver my baby knowing she is already gone? I will never get to look into her eyes and tell her how much I loved her and how much she means to me, to be able to tell her the immense joy she brought me during these past nine months. I will never get to watch her take those precious first wobbly steps or hear that magical word, momma.*

I felt robbed, robbed of everything we had dreamed about these past nine months.

Arriving at the front door to the hospital I went through the motions of checking in, filling out the forms and then we were taken to the far end of the hallway to a private room which I was thankful for.

The nurses told me that I could have this room for the duration of my stay there and that I wouldn't have to be moved to the delivery room where there were moms with their happy, healthy newborns. I was induced at 10am and labored fairly effortlessly through the afternoon until around 4pm when the contractions became more intense. I was promised the relief of drugs when I felt I needed them. I asked for an epidural in the late afternoon and within a few minutes felt the bliss of the icy medication running down my spine numbing the pain, echoing the numbness I felt in my heart.

I was lucky to have had two of the most amazing nurses looking after me that awful day. They stayed with me, held my hand and answered the many questions I had about the unfolding events and what to expect (as they had helped with previous stillbirths before). Their comforting, loving nature helped give me the strength I needed to get through birthing a baby I knew we would never get to bring home with us.

Finally after her clinic hours were over, my doctor returned in the evening and increased the dosage of the medication, making the contractions more intense and closer together. I vividly remember just minutes before the birth, the uncontrollable shaking of my legs. I was suddenly very cold and I could not make my legs be still, the nurse told me it was shock. She put a hospital blanket over me that had come directly out of the warmer which calmed the shakes. The delivery itself went quite quickly, a couple of pushes and she was out.

At approximately 11:10pm on Wednesday, May 10th, 2006; just four short days before what would have been our first Mother's Day together, our daughter Emily Megan was born.

There were no tears of joy, only an eerie, suffocating silence that filled the room. She never got to draw a breath, we knew we would never hear her cry.

She was whisked away to the next room for an examination and when the doctor returned she told my husband and I that from a visual exam she could find nothing wrong with the baby only that the cord had been wrapped tightly around her neck, terming the death an umbilical cord accident. With that being said, my doctor patted me on the thigh and said only five words to me, "try to get some rest" and walked quickly out the door.

To this day I am still hurt by that. There were no words of comfort, no sympathies. I guess I just needed to feel like after all we had been through together, that Emily and I had meant something to her, meant something more than a pat on the leg after the trauma of delivering a stillborn baby. I often wonder if it was just that as a professional she had to distance herself from tragedy like this; that it was also painful for her. That perhaps she, after performing so many of these devastating deliveries, dealt with it in her own way, away from the patient. I am sure that if doctors became involved on a personal level with each couple who has experienced a loss, it would tear them apart as well. To this day it is still something neither of us has ever brought up or discussed.

In talking with doctors and others, I managed to gather that a Cord Accident generally refers to something having disrupted the blood flow to the baby through its cord. A cord accident might be due to the umbilical cord becoming tangled or knotted, cutting off the baby's blood supply, or it might mean the cord itself couldn't sustain the pregnancy because of medical factors. I was told that it could happen from having a cord that was very long or not long enough. Regardless, if anything happens to the cord prohibiting the nutrients and oxygen from reaching the baby it can cause a cord accident.

In our case, all the doctor could find was that the cord wrapped tightly several times around her little neck. She said to us that with the occurrence of most stillbirths the actual cause would likely never be known for certain. I was told it was nothing I had done nor could have done to prevent it from happening, it is a *silent killer.* Within a mere week of the previous check–up, she quietly slipped away from us, undetected, gone forever.

CHAPTER 6

Emily was brought in to spend some time with us during the night. We heard the *whoosh* of the door as it opened. We were nervous and frightened, not knowing what to expect when we saw her for the first time.

The nurse slowly entered carrying a pink, striped bundle and gently placed her in my husband's arms. We were taken aback at just how heavy and still she was. Darren and I sat on my bed together and held her. She was truly beautiful and looked like she was just asleep, resting peacefully. She was so perfect, ten teeny, tiny little fingers and toes. Gorgeous, fine, reddish–blonde wisps of peach fuzz peeking out from underneath the knitted pink hat they had gingerly placed on her head. Her tiny, full delicate lips were a startling bright red. On her cheek and tiny foot, a small red, 'rashy' patch that indicated to the doctor that she may have been gone longer than the couple of days we had originally thought.We sat there as the hours passed holding our Emily, telling her how much we had wanted her, loved her, studying every inch of her, not wanting to forget a thing about this precious angel. I don't even remember what time it was when the nurse came to take her away.

That was the one and only time we saw her.

Morning fell, breakfasts were delivered and everyone else was going on with their normal day. I was still laying in the same bed I had, just hours before, delivered my stillborn baby girl in. I fell in and out of sleep that morning, hearing from a distance people coming in and out of the room wanting to talk about what we were doing with the body . . . the body? All that kept running through my mind was that my daughter is being referred to as 'a body' and now we, as her parents, had to make a decision about what we wanted to do with her. It felt like a nightmare I was desperate to wake from. We were brought in a package of poems about baby angels but what we needed at that time was information about all the things we had to do and how to go about getting the services we needed.

My husband and I discussed it and decided we would have her cremated and scatter her ashes in a place special to us.

We signed the release papers to have the funeral home pick her up and transport her to the crematorium and then prepared to leave the hospital and return home.

We walked to the nursing station to let them know we were leaving and to hand off other forms we needed to have filled out. We walked past the rooms of the smiling, happy parents, hearing the cries of their healthy babies. The nurses buzzed around, in and out of their rooms offering advice and assistance with breastfeeding issues and colicky babies. I wanted to make it all go away, I wanted my baby with me the way it was supposed to be.

I honestly don't remember how I found the strength to walk out of that building that day and leave our baby behind. I thought of how in the grand scheme of life, no parent should ever have to outlive their child, babies are not supposed to die.

My husband took my hand and we never looked back.

CHAPTER 7

Heavy–hearted; we began the journey home, the journey we had been anticipating for nine long months. Only now our dream of bringing our little one home to complete our family was shattered. Our little Emily was not coming home.

Silence echoed through the van, sadness filled our souls and the empty void in the backseat where we had lovingly installed the brand new infant car seat just a week before now seemed suddenly larger than life.

We returned home around supper time and as we pulled up to the house I felt a rush of emotions flood over me; numbness, despair, fear, panic, exhaustion. I tried my very best to put on a brave face for my two kids and my mom who were waiting for us. We had been in the door for no more than ten minutes when the nurse from our local health unit called to schedule a home visit to talk about the stillbirth. I didn't want to see anyone, talk to anyone or have anyone hug me and tell me how sorry they were, because I knew then I would lose any control I did have. I wanted to be strong for everyone. This array of emotions mixed with the physical pain of the birth itself and the hormones wreaking havoc on my body and mind seemed too much to bear. I was angry at my body for allowing such a cruel and horrific thing happen to my baby. To the body, a birth is a birth, it is not aware that there is no baby anymore, no baby that needs to be fed or cared for. It just continues to carry on doing its job of producing milk and healing to its pre-pregnancy state. I was coming home with empty arms that were aching to hold Emily, a heart shredded into a million pieces and I still had to go through the same healing as a "happy, normal" mommy.

I took the folic acid before conceiving, I took care of myself, eating healthy for two. For heaven's sake, I could hardly bring myself to take a simple pain relief pill (deemed safe) throughout the entire pregnancy, so how could this have possibly happened? I did everything right. I did everything, and more, just like the multitude of other mommies around me; only I didn't get to bring my sweet baby home.

I was battling between anger, numbness and heartbreak as I settled in at home and began the powerful grieving process.

The one thing that brought me immediate comfort was to be back with my children. Their smiles and excited stories of their day managed to bring a smile to my face. I just wanted to hold them and forget the pain of the nightmare we had all lived through the past few days. To this day, everyday, I am so thankful for them.

As the following days turned into weeks, the long journey of healing began. The beautiful cradle, the baby car seat, the delicate little pink dresses and sleepers, all put away in the basement for storage. All traces of the months of excited planning and hopeful dreams being fulfilled with her homecoming were hidden away in hopes that if perhaps maybe we didn't see them, it wouldn't hurt so much. Their absence mirrored the huge void in our hearts.

Some days were easier than others. For the first few weeks I had difficulty seeing past the fog that clouded my aching heart. I put myself into a kind of self quarantine, the house being a safe place for me. I could talk to my caring friends who were calling to check on me, if I was ready. If I was not feeling up to it or unable to, Darren would go to the door, fill them in and accept their cards or gifts.

I was actually quite surprised at how quickly I suddenly wanted to talk about her, after the birth, to share with my kids the memories we did have. The times of her 'playing' with them, when they had their little hands on my belly, surprising them with her kicks as they laughed in delight. It made her 'more real' and even though she will never be here with us I wanted them to always remember she was still, and will forever be, a part of our family.

My mom, a teacher at the same school I worked at, would come everyday after school bearing the gift of an incredibly delicious meal donated from members of the staff who had so generously signed up to feed my family for the first couple of weeks of my homecoming. These amazing, caring people ensured we had full meals and that we were taken care of everyday, complete with fruit and goody baskets sent from both mine and Darren's workplaces.

We are very fortunate to live in such a warm and caring community. People we hadn't seen in a long time showed up at the door with cards of sympathy, a pan of lasagna, beautiful flowers or a warm hug. For this we will be eternally grateful. Cards were pouring in at the post office box with loving wishes of prayers and sympathy for our family.

One card in particular touched me incredibly. It was sent from a friend in town, who had lost her sweet baby girl just four months earlier to a heart problem. She reached out to me in my time of great need and offered a walk or talk when I was ready. Desperate to talk to and be with someone who truly knew the depth of the pain I was in and with whom I could talk openly and frankly, I called her the same day. We went for a small walk on a local trail and I vividly remember that as being the day the fog slowly began to lift from my heart. It was so therapeutic for me to be able to be totally and completely open, sharing the stories of the losses of our baby girls, talking about things you just couldn't discuss with anyone else, things nobody wanted to hear. With Christine I didn't have to hide behind a smile and say that everything was okay, when it really wasn't. She knew better. It was okay to talk about things others would find too morbid; but to us, it was just life. Over the course of that summer we shared the bond of our new found special relationship. Our times together were a much needed break in my world, especially when I became overwhelmed with sadness, watching from within my bubble, all the other happy, blissful mommies holding their precious little bundles or pushing them in their strollers. That was supposed to be me, it just hurt so much to see.

CHAPTER 8

It was a dark time for me, that beautiful spring. I felt like I could not feel the warmth of the sun or see the beauty around me. I did not want to open the blinds and let the light in. I took little enjoyment gardening in my backyard or in the beauty of my flowers. I really could have cared less that year, it just meant nothing.

I replayed over and over in my head the day of Emily's birth, every detail, every second etched in my memory. I would "rewind" images in my mind as if watching a movie and play it over again.

One thing that gave me a little solace and brought a smile to my heart happened one day when I had asked for a sign that my little Emily was okay, that she was safe where she was now. The very next day I was sitting in my living room, looking out the patio window, and a tiny, beautiful, white butterfly flew past. It fluttered right in front of the window and then back and

29

forth again. My first instinct was to dismiss any significance of meaning to its sudden arrival. But, my little butterfly 'dropped by' every day that summer and continued to return. Where ever I was, I could see this delicate, white butterfly. I like to believe that it was her little spirit appearing to bring me comfort and let me know she was just fine. Assuring me, that even though I would never be able to hold her again, she was still here with me. Where ever I may be, to this very day, all I have to do is look around and I can always see my little butterfly with me. I smile thinking of her.

I became obsessed with becoming pregnant again. I had been told by the doctor that after having one or two normal cycles return we would be able to try again. So began the desperate praying to get a menstrual period back. The same period I, ironically, had prayed every month before not to come in the hopes of being pregnant and then despised so vehemently upon its arrival.

People would excitedly tell me about friends or co-workers who were now pregnant, very innocently or unknowingly not realizing the pain it caused to a mommy who was still grieving the loss of her own newborn baby.

Don't get me wrong, I was genuinely so very happy for them. I truly believe a pregnancy and baby is a blessing, the most precious gift anyone can receive. This experience we were living through made that crystal clear to me but it hurt, a lot. It was a reminder of what I had just lost and wanted so desperately to have. I became angry at myself for having those feelings, my sadness and grief at times turned to resentment and heartache.

I was consumed with *why*; Why me? Why did she have to die? Why does it seem so easy for everyone around me to get pregnant and deliver a healthy baby that they get to bring home?

It was about a month before I was able to venture out and back into the 'real world', so to speak. Every time I prepared to leave the house I would ask for strength to make it through the day without breaking down. Crying, for me, was something I didn't want to do in front of others. I did my crying at night, when it was quiet, everyone was tucked away in bed and I was alone. That is when the tears silently rolled down my cheeks, sometimes overflowing to sobs as I would remember my longing for and love of Emily.

Going out and seeing the look on many people's faces often made me feel like I was out on display, almost like you could hear the whispers; "She's the one who lost her baby" or "I can't imagine what she's going through, poor girl." I felt the stares of pity as I walked down the street or through the stores.

I felt awful thinking about the fourth grade students I had worked with at school who had shared in the excitement of my pregnancy through each stage. I was consumed with guilt that this would cause them pain and confusion. Having a baby is supposed to be a happy, joyous occasion, not a time to try to explain to them why Mrs. Anderson didn't come home with her baby. Every so often I look through the beautiful book of condolences the class had written and sent to me after I returned home from the hospital. It still manages to bring a smile to my face and a little tear to my eye as I think of how wonderful those children were and how much it meant to me.

CHAPTER 9

To my sheer amazement, I found out late that summer that I was pregnant again, total bliss and excitement! I was in shock over how quickly it happened and I consistently worried even though the HCG blood testing I did every few days was showing a rise; which is a good indicator of a strong pregnancy. I had some joy again and went forward with some new found hope although we had told only a couple of people due to my apprehension. I had a kind of 'guarded' excitement deep down inside but it never felt quite right. I worried constantly that it had happened too soon, that maybe my body wasn't totally healed and ready to support another pregnancy yet.

I returned to work that September although the pain of our loss had not gone away, and it never will, but things became a little more manageable, a little easier. That was until devastation struck again. Later that month, I awoke one night with some bleeding which sent me packing to the local emergency room in fear. The doctor on call said that there was not much that they could do besides call my doctor on Monday and get an ultrasound done to check if everything was ok, then I was sent home.

The cramping and pain became more intense throughout the evening as did the bleeding and it became evident that I was having a miscarriage. During that awful night, after only a few early weeks, my husband and I lost another tiny life.

The following day once again, off to the hospital we went for an emergency ultrasound only to find that I had indeed had a spontaneous and complete miscarriage. I threw myself right back to work the next day, sad, frustrated and back at square one again. I was angry with my body, with myself, wondering why after having two non-eventful pregnancies and safe deliveries in the past with my two older children, why I couldn't have a baby now? I lived for the hope that maybe next month would be the one to answer my dream; that it would finally again be MY turn.

CHAPTER 10

Seeing new babies and pregnant bellies continued to be too much for me. There were times at work when I had to make a quick exit into the bathroom or dash into an empty classroom while I tried my best to fight back the hot, wet tears stinging my eyes. The sight of a new mom with her happy, cherub baby invoked panic deep within me. Seeing a cuddly, cooing baby being passed around the room as everyone waited their turn to hold him or her sent a sharp, searing pain right to my heart. Again, a reminder that I too should have a baby, that was supposed to be me too.

I was even unable to attend baby showers, others not able to understand why I would politely decline the invitations. I felt like people maybe thought enough time had passed and I should be getting 'over it' and moving on. It just wasn't that easy for me. As much as I would have liked to be there to celebrate and welcome a beautiful little one to the world, I just wasn't ready; it was still too painful. It took me a long time to even be comfortable holding a baby again, something that always made me feel badly. As time passed and my healing progressed, it became easier for me.

Every month that went by became more frustrating than the last as I would come to find that once again, I was not pregnant. It became a quest, a yearning for my dream of having my own baby to come true once again. It was around this time that we invested in what I had hoped to be the 'miracle cure'; a home ovulation monitor. I had heard of its success from another girlfriend and she swore by it. I figured it was worth a try at least. I faithfully did my stick dipping every day that the machine asked for it but to no avail. At the end of every cycle I was greeted by my period, again.

After several months of unsuccessful trying and what felt like hundreds of dollars spent on negative HPT's (I should've had the wisdom of purchasing stocks in the company!) I finally gave in and fled to the doctor in tears, begging for help. She did a blood workup to check hormone levels and low and behold, my FSH (follicle stimulating hormone) levels, necessary for ovulation and in turn pregnancy, were almost non-existent! All these months that passed and the emotional roller coaster I rode every month was for nothing,

I had never even been ovulating. Now It became apparent why the home monitor wasn't able to give an accurate result!

My doctor, understanding of my frustration and urgency, prescribed two rounds of medication in hopes of boosting ovulation. She tried to reassure me that it *would* happen and gave me words of encouragement and support to persevere. After completing the second round on July 24th, 2007; the eve of our third anniversary also became a momentous day as my friend Christine delivered a healthy, beautiful baby girl. My heart surged with joy for her and her family, what a precious gift!

To add even more wonder to an already amazing day, after returning home from my part time summer job, on a whim, I decided to take another HPT (even though I knew I was still early by two days!) There were no words to describe the absolute elation of seeing that second pink line creep across the testing window!

I stared in disbelief. I think I stared at that stick for hours, making sure my eyes were not playing a trick on me, then I ran to get the camera! (This picture is, in fact, the first one in the baby book!)

It was a night filled with surprise and wonderful news that will always hold special memories for me. I will never forget that day!

CHAPTER 11

The next few weeks were filled with frequent trips to the hospital lab where I anxiously and excitedly had HCG testing done to monitor the rising levels. It was something my doctor did for my benefit to help me feel a little stronger about the validity of this pregnancy. At around the nine week mark, I was able to have an ultrasound to check for a heartbeat. Once again, with every emotion running through my mind, I lay on that table beside that same kind and gentle technician. As she put the warm gel on my belly and ran the wand across there was silence, deafening silence until I heard those amazing words, "There is a heartbeat!" She gave me a hug as I was leaving and told me how truly happy she was for me.

I tried to take one day at a time for the next few months, one milestone to another, one appointment to the next. I delayed telling others of our newfound joy, in fear of losing another tiny life. It was not until well into the second trimester that I was confident enough to share our news. I had heard the heartbeat and seen the baby, perfectly formed and strong. It was not until then that I was able to relax, a little, and believe it was real. A struggle for me was to try not to compare the two pregnancies in morbid fear of having a repeated ending like that of Emily's pregnancy. Everyday I had to remind myself that this time was going to be different. That it was a new little life growing inside of me that I was allowed to love and be excited for and that it was okay to feel these feelings again.

This pregnancy went a lot more smoothly until October hit and we received the devastating news from Darren's sister that his mother's brave battle with breast cancer was coming to an end. She had been given two weeks, to a month, to live.

On November 28th, the day after my older daughter's birthday, surrounded by her family of loved ones, a truly remarkable and amazing woman quietly passed away. We had spent three days camped out in the hospital to be with her. Everyone in the family taking shifts to be with her so she would never be left alone. Her last wish, and only request, was that someone always be there with her to hold her hand.

The last thing she told my husband was that she wanted him to take care of the baby growing inside of me. She called it the "special baby" and told him how she knew in her heart that this baby would bring happiness to the family after she was gone.

Her death continues to weigh heavily on all our hearts, our biggest regret being that she would never get to see or hold our "special" baby.

CHAPTER 12

Everyday I tried my very best to maintain a positive attitude, throwing myself into my family, my children and their activities. Excitedly cheering them on through swim meets, soccer and hockey games, taking great joy and pride in what incredible kids they are and how much I loved them. We had family movie nights, game nights and special times that we treasured and that drew us all even closer together through this tough time.

Christmas came and went and we rang in 2008 with great anticipation of receiving the greatest gift, our living baby. My original due date was slated for April 1st, but after our previous loss my doctor, the same doctor who had seen me through the first pregnancy and delivery and who knew well my medical history, decided that if I went to Edmonton for an amniocentesis and providing that the lungs were developed fully, she would induce and deliver this baby at thirty-six weeks. A week earlier than Emily's sudden, tragic death. In an effort to ease my mind, wrought with worry on a daily basis, my doctor allowed for extra ultrasounds and often took calls personally from me at the end of her work day.

My husband and I were torn as to whether we wanted to find out the sex of this baby this time. I was SO ready to find out! I often teased him that since I always got to go into the ultrasound first, while all the measurements were being taken, that I would find out and not tell him! He was very adamant that this time we would not find out, either of us. He insisted that since we had waited this long, we could wait until the end and have a true gift. Neither of us truly cared what sex this baby was as long as it was safe, healthy and that we actually got to bring this one home with us.

It was around this same time that I had managed to find a wonderful doctor and clinic nurse here in town who were very reassuring and understanding of my fears and anxieties. The loving, gentle nurse allowed me to come into the clinic, at any time. She would take me into a little room at the back of the office and pull out the hand held doppler and we would both smile as we heard the comforting heartbeat just a beating away. She was truly my angel and helped more than she will ever know, getting me through to the end.

I left my job at the school on Valentine's Day and began preparations, yet again, to hopefully bring our baby home.

As a family, we were beginning to allow ourselves to get a little excited. The kids were looking forward to having the new baby home but felt very apprehensive and guarded as well. They, like Darren and I, would not truly be able to believe it until the baby was delivered safe and healthy. We tried to include them in appointments and visits to the clinics where they were able to hear the heartbeat or see the tiny image of their brother or sister on the ultrasound. Anything to help reassure their minds that everything was being done this time. That this time, everyone was taking every precaution so nothing bad would happen to our baby again.

The next few weeks were abuzz with weekly visits to the doctor, ultrasounds, and the appointment I dreaded the most, the amniocentesis in the city! With happy thoughts and a brave face we packed up our bags, installed our little infant car seat (again) and headed to the big city at thirty–six weeks. I battled my fear of having them stick that 'big' needle into my belly to see if my baby's lungs were fully developed.

At the previous weeks appointment with my own doctor we had a plan formulated that after having the procedure done we would stop at the hospital an hour away from home on our long four hour trip home from Edmonton. My doctor would have the results phoned to her at the hospital later that day.

I was pleasantly surprised that the amniocentesis went very smoothly. I had agonized repeatedly over having the procedure done and it was over in less than five minutes! I had heard terrible stories of the pain and horror of it and had worried myself into a fit over it. The doctor there was wonderful and after a quick look at the ultrasound, he inserted the thin needle into my enormous belly ever so gently and withdrew the amniotic fluid. It was actually very painless.

I tried to see the whole thing as just being one step closer to the day I would hold my sweet baby.

When we arrived at my own doctor's hospital, she met us there. She entered the room we were seated in, waiting for the positive news that we would have this baby that day. As she walked in, her head hung, we knew right away the results were not what we had hoped. The lungs were not quite fully mature and she could not deliver that day. The good news from the specialist was that in one week it would be safe to deliver. However, as she said, that was also the week of our loss of our sweet Emily just two years earlier. She told me she knew how difficult living through this next week would be but arranged for me to go for daily non stress tests at our local hospital, which gave me great relief. With that being said, she came over, reached out and gave me a warm hug. A hug I whole heartedly embraced, wishing that we had had that connection two years earlier after the stillbirth, when I felt I needed it the most. I hoped she knew just how much that meant to me, and still does to this very day.

The times that I had arranged to go for my non-stress tests were precious moments each day. In the peaceful, dimly lit room I could focus solely on the joyous, blissful sound of my baby's heart beating, a comforting and very reassuring sound. It gave me the strength to hope and believe that the end was so close now, and that everything would be okay this time.

CHAPTER 13

On a sunny and somewhat warm morning on March 12th, 2008, ironically a Wednesday, the same day and practically the same time as I gave birth nearly two years before, we arrived at that same hospital to have our baby.

The first thing they did was to hook me up to the fetal monitor and we heard that familiar little heart beating strongly. I received the induction to start the process of delivery. I just wanted to be able to return to that hospital and have a good experience, for everyone involved. I wanted to go back and have a living baby, dissolving my fear of that hospital being a bad place, the place where bad things happened to my babies.

I had gentle, somewhat easy contractions for most of the afternoon until around 4pm when they became very strong very quickly! My doctor was called in to do an emergency C-Section on the woman labouring in the next room, so when she popped her head in, I told her that I was desperate for drugs, I was so ready for that heavenly epidural! She told me she would return quickly after her section, examine me and then get the anesthesiologist to get it going. I waited for quite some time with contractions coming hard and heavy, one minute apart. One on top of the other with no relief in between to recover and focus.

When I heard her at the door, talking with a nurse, I don't think I had ever been so happy to hear anyone's voice before! Within a few minutes time, I went from being somewhat out of control from the pain, to feeling like a brand new woman once I received that epidural. Life was good now! The pain was gone and I was able to relax and concentrate on finally meeting our very long awaited baby.

Around 10:30pm the nurse and doctor came in to check on the progress of things and asked if I was feeling any pressure, I had indeed been feeling it for the last half hour or so. Upon the final exam the doctor looked at me and said, "Ok, let's have this baby," and left the room to get prepared.

The atmosphere in the room was light and filled with excitement. She asked me for one push and after that within seconds she had pulled the baby out and was clamping the cord. It was all happening so fast! My husband was able to cut the cord and the baby was cleaned off and put on my belly. I felt an immense rush of happiness wash instantly over me. I was overwhelmed with love and amazement that the baby was right here and everything was okay. I remember hearing those three blissful words I had waited so long to hear. With a big smile the doctor announced, "It's a BOY!"

I have vivid memories of holding him for the first time and looking into those big, beautiful, blue eyes that were staring up at me; hearing that amazing cry as he drew his first breath coming into this world healthy and safe.

And so, at 11:15pm, our gorgeous little boy, Brennan Matthew completed our loving family.

When we were wheeled to our private room the doctor came in to check on us before leaving for the night. She told us the news of what I had feared throughout this entire pregnancy that Brennan had been born with the umbilical cord wrapped around his neck. The same reason that we lost our little Emily, and made me instantly feel eternally grateful for the gift of this healthy little boy laying in my arms.

I knew in my heart that we had two very special angels watching over us that day. They were there to make sure Brennan arrived safely. Although he will never meet his Grandma or his big sister Emily, I felt them both with us the night he was born.

I don't think I closed my eyes at all the first few nights, terrified that if I did, something terrible may happen to him. I remember staring at him in awe, trying to come to terms that he was completely fine and healthy and safe.

My nightmare was over. My fear of losing another tiny baby finally dissolved as a new sense of peace washed over me.

CHAPTER 14

He will never take the place of our little Emily, nor was he ever meant to, but I knew he would bring such tremendous joy to our broken hearts.

Watching him grow and change into the gorgeous, free spirited bundle of energy he is fills my heart with love each and every day! He is a lucky little boy to have older siblings who live and breathe him, who love him so fiercely; in addition to having a great big family full of people who adore him with all their hearts.

Emily will always be with us in our hearts and hold a special place in our family. Even though I can't hold her or kiss her beautiful little face ever again or tell her how happy or lucky I was to be able to be her mommy even for such a short time, she remains a part of me forever.

On a daily basis I am reminded of her death. When I see other little girls her age outside playing, holding their mommy's hand, I can't help but wonder who she would look like now. Would she be shy and quiet or giggly and adventurous? There is not a day that passes without thinking about how much I miss her dearly. I often feel a little tear well up inside me when I see the beautiful smile of a little girl with her mommy.

I have accepted that she is gone and know that her birth and death happened for a reason. Perhaps maybe one day I will be able to see that reason more clearly and understand why.

For now I do know that she has made me a stronger person and has drawn my husband, my family and I closer together as we all searched for answers on the road towards some kind of healing. Living through our loss has made me truly thankful for life's gifts; no matter how simple or grand. Life's lessons have taught me to embrace each day, for you never know just what tomorrow will bring.

CHAPTER 15

After the heart wrenching loss of a much loved baby or pregnancy at any stage, you may face a rush of many powerful emotions as you begin to travel the lonely path of sadness and grief in hopes of finding some inner peace and understanding. Know you are not alone in your grief. The fact is that too many of us have had to take that journey, too many of us parents have angels in heaven and not in our arms. None the less, we are *still* mommies, *still* parents. The love we carry for our sweet babies in our hearts everyday will continue to live on forever.

Often parents may feel the urge to try again for another baby after a loss. Some want to begin trying as soon as physically is possible. While for others, they need more time to heal. For some, the trauma may just be so great and it is too scary to try again. It is a very emotional and personal decision that has no right or wrong answer. You may wonder, is another pregnancy possible, will it ever happen for me? In most cases it is possible after the devastation of your loss. For some, such as myself, there may be some stumbling blocks on the road to reaching that ultimate goal of a pregnancy that ends in you bringing home your healthy, thriving baby. Don't be afraid to seek help from your doctor if after a few months of trying you feel something may be wrong. I am living proof it can happen!

Making the difficult decision of wanting to try again takes a lot of courage and strength, for those of us who have experienced the loss of a baby at any stage know what can happen, what can go wrong. For us, another pregnancy carries overwhelming emotions from start to finish, this is perfectly normal. For me there was no more carefree, innocent bliss and excitement, but rather my subsequent pregnancy was filled with guarded anticipation and worry throughout. I remember many times where a twinge of pain or a lack of 'normal' movement would send me into a full panic. Every day I just prayed that this time everything would be okay. I clung to the hope that in the end I would hold this healthy, beautiful baby and bring it home with us. I heard repeatedly, "You just have to relax." I knew, of course, this was meant very sincerely, but that was not something that was ever helpful or realistic to me. I understood that for my own health and my future baby's health that it was important to try but once someone has experienced a loss of a child, no matter how hard you try, it is just not that easy; not until the baby is delivered safely and is placed in the arms of its very anxious parents.

I believe your heart will guide you in knowing when you are ready to try again and will give you hope and faith as you go through the following fearful months ahead. I found solace in connecting with others going through the same situation; reading and just talking with my friend, helped to calm my fears and make it one step to the next.

Allow yourself as much time as you need to grieve the loss of your baby. Don't be ashamed to cry and cry often, every one of your feelings is so very valid and plays an important part in your grieving process. I was told once that as the tears begin to flow, the healing has begun. There are no timelines or emotional deadlines you should feel you have to meet during your journey from the dark fog to finding some peace and moving forward. Take every day, every situation one day at a time and do what feels right for you. Know that everyone grieves in their own way and that there is no right or wrong way to mourn your loss. Others may offer well meaning tips of advice for you in efforts to help you get through this time. It's a different process for each person and some things may just not seem right for you, that's okay too.

You may find it helpful to take others up on their offers of help, anything to make the daily routine easier for you. You will have one less thing to worry about and you can better focus on taking care of yourself. Consider having a member of your family or a close friend who is willing to act as a 'spokesman', someone that anyone who is worried about you can contact, rather than you having to deal with phone call after phone call when you may just want to be left alone. Some days it might just be too hard to keep repeating yourself over to each new caller, to answer questions about the birth, the baby and how you are coping. It will allow you to handle talking to others when you are emotionally ready to do so, instead of having to relive the experience every time the phone rings.

My suggestion to you is to read. Read whatever you can and take comfort and hope in other's stories and successes. Search the internet, the library or talk to your local health nurse or doctor. They may be able to give you some reading or suggestions on helpful information. You may also seek comfort from a local support group. There you will be able to openly share your feelings and special memories with others who can totally understand the depth of your emotions and can offer a wealth of information on how they have coped with their losses. They may also have a library of resources on many issues and topics or even newsletters that you will find very helpful.

Try to remember the special bond you did have with your baby, the happy memories of hearing that first heartbeat or feeling that familiar little kick from inside you. From day one, your precious little one was loved and special, carry those treasures close to your heart and in time, they will become happier memories.

Talk to others around you when you feel ready to. It is surprising when you open up and share your story with others the amount of times you will hear, "I lost a baby as well", or "My friend had the same thing happen to her", all from the most unlikely of people. People that, in hearing your story, will reveal their own painful journeys and you will soon discover just how often lives have been touched by the loss of a baby. To connect with other bereaved parents, for me, was like being given a gift. A gift of comfort and understanding. It offers a chance to share your special memories of your beautiful baby. Something that is so important as our memories are often all we may have to hold on to.

You may find that many people just don't know what to say to you after the loss of your baby. They don't know if it's okay to hug you or to talk about your baby in front of you. Some may feel like they have to 'walk on eggshells' around you or not say anything at all in hopes of not upsetting you. For some, it is just too uncomfortable to deal with and they may avoid talking to you at all. Let them know that you want to talk about your baby, a baby that is always going to be a special part of you forever. Mention your baby's name, let them know you want your baby's life and spirit to be remembered.

Don't be afraid to ask questions of any doctor you choose to see. It is your right to be comfortable and to receive the utmost excellence in prenatal care. Make a list of any and all questions you have and bring them to your doctor's appointment. It may be beneficial to book an extended session with the doctor to ensure you get all your questions answered without being rushed out the door. This is especially important during the six week postnatal check up. I found this tip to be very helpful at my check up where we discussed my volumes of questions and concerns about a subsequent pregnancy. We were able to talk through finding out about the stillbirth, the difficult delivery and my healing process at that time.

Make sure your doctor understands any relevant history of your loss, especially important if you have switched doctors. Ensure they are willing to give you any measures of comfort you may feel you need in another pregnancy, such as an opportunity to come in and listen to the baby's heartbeat when you are feeling very anxious. (It is also possible to rent personal dopplers over the internet for your own sanity and peace of mind to use at home.)

Be strong. The power of positive thinking is truly amazing! Say to yourself often, I will have a beautiful, healthy baby to bring home. Don't be afraid to be excited about reaching milestones in your pregnancy. While it's perfectly normal and okay to be scared or terrified of another loss, try to let yourself bond with the new life growing inside of you. Do special things for yourself during this time, treat yourself to something that makes you feel really good and uplifts your spirits, you deserve that! Surround yourself with love and support from positive people around you. Feel in your heart that good things are coming as you wait for that magical day when you will finally be able to hold your new baby in your arms, look down at that gorgeous little face and know that everything is right with the world again.

In reading this book, it is my wish that you have found some faith, hope, and some useful information from my experience as you look forward to the future and to what lies ahead for you in your healing.

I found the old saying, 'time heals all wounds' to be somewhat true. As time passes, the rawness of your pain will subside and things may seem a little easier to cope with. Although it will never completely go away, remembering the precious

time and special memories you did share with
your baby will, in time, bring happiness to your
now aching heart.

May you be blessed as you travel the journey
of grief and healing. My thoughts and prayers are
with you now and always.

CHAPTER 16

That is my story. Along the way my family and I lived through a tragedy no parent should ever have to face, the excruciating pain of losing a child. I found deep within myself new strength and had to learn how to move forward, to go on without my little girl.

My hope is that in Emily's death, her little legacy lives on by offering comfort and peace to other parents facing adversities in their struggle to move forth after the devastation and unspeakable pain of losing a baby.

Thank you for sharing my family's journey of life's trials, heartache, grief, healing and hope as, together, we moved forward living through the unbearable heartbreak of . . . *Losing Emily.*

I wanted to share with you a beautiful poem I found on the internet that both warmed my heart and gave me comfort and peace. May it touch you as deeply as it did me.

AN ANGEL
NEVER DIES

Don't let them say I wasn't born,
That something stopped my heart
I felt each tender squeeze you gave,
I've loved you from the start.

Although my body you can't hold
It doesn't mean I'm gone
This world was worthy, not of me
God chose that I move on.

I know the pain that drowns your soul,
What you are forced to face
You have my word, I'll fill your arms,
Someday we will embrace.

You'll hear that it was meant to be,
God doesn't make mistakes
But that wont soften your worst blow,
Or make your heart not ache.

I'm watching over all you do,
Another child you'll bear
Believe me when I say to you,
That I am always there.

There will come a time, I promise you,
When you will hold my hand,
Stroke my face and kiss my lips
And then you'll understand.

Although I've never breathed your air,
Or gazed into your eyes

That doesn't mean I never was,
An Angel never dies.

—Author unknown

Unknown Author. Online posting. Viewed 23 June
2009.   http://www.powyssands.org/poems.htm.
Used with permission from SANDS (Stillbirth and
Neonatal Death Charity) 2009. www.powyssands.org
    * Special thanks going to Shirley (Powy Sands)
for allowing me to share this powerful poem.

I also discovered a website filled with many beautiful, touching poems on the loss of a baby. Too many to mention each one by name, but I took great comfort in the words written from other grieving parents. It is a beautiful tribute to so many little angels lost. It showed me I was not alone in my grief, that there were countless others out there sharing the same pain. http://www.honoredbabies.org/writing-center/poetry.   Used with permission from Paula Long. (2009)

www.honoredbabies.org

WITH SPECIAL THANKS

We feel that we have been truly blessed with the gift of having so many amazing people in our lives.

Thank you to all of our loving, supportive families from both near and far, each one of you means the world to us. Without you, we are nothing.

To our parents who have always been there for us unconditionally, we love you. To our incredible children; Chris, Kaitlyn, Chase and Brennan, each one of you gives us immense joy and fills us with love and pride every day.

We are so grateful to have such a vast array of wonderful friends who have reached out to us during the nightmare of losing our little daughter. Your caring got us through many difficult times. For every card or beautiful arrangement of flowers sent, filled with loving wishes of sympathy, for every gift of food or help offered to us, for every smile and hug, or simply just being there and listening when I was ready to talk; thank you from the bottom of my heart.

To anyone who reached out to our family, you will never know how much even the smallest of gestures has touched our hearts forever.

A very special thank you going to our doctor for seeing us through that chapter in our lives and helping us to safely bring home our "special baby". A truly phenomenal gift we treasure each and every day. Thank you for putting up with my frazzled mind, wrought consistently with worry and fear, until you placed that healthy little boy in my arms! We will never forget you.

Thank you to the multitude of wonderful nurses at both hospitals. Thank you for taking such special care of all of us. For every nurse who helped wipe a tear or shared a warm smile or words of encouragement, your kindness and gentle, loving manner touched us deeply during our time of need.

To Christine, whose offering of a special newfound friendship, as you were grieving your own traumatic loss, got me through many difficult times. I can never thank you enough for taking my hand and making me feel like I was not alone. There are no words that express how much I truly appreciated every talk, every hug, each word of support and guidance that helped me to work through the heartache of the grieving process. I will always treasure our times together. Your strength and courage showed me that there is a light at the end of that dark road of unknowns. I am, and will forever be, so very thankful for you coming into my life.

Lastly, to my husband, you always have been, and always will be my rock. Thank you for always being there for me, for sharing your strength, love, patience and unwavering support every day. I love you with all of my soul.

ABOUT THE AUTHOR

Tammy Anderson lives amidst the beauty of the Rocky Mountains in Jasper, Alberta with her husband Darren, and her three wonderful children. Together they enjoy hockey, basketball, swimming, golfing and traveling. Above all, they treasure just being together and spending time as a family.

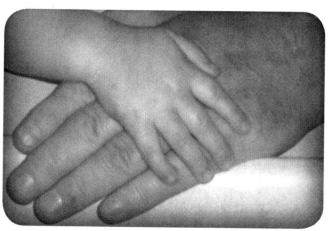

T. Anderson, 2009

Sept. 2010

LaVergne, TN USA
04 August 2010

192053LV00002B/2/P

9 781592 99460